Infant Bonds of Joy

Also by Roger Weingarten

INFANT BONDS OF JOY

POEMS BY

Roger Weingarten

David R. Godine · Publisher
BOSTON

For Ellen, Eli, and Jonah

First published in 1990 by
David R. Godine, Publisher, Inc.
Horticultural Hall
300 Massachusetts Avenue
Boston, Massachusetts 02115

ISBN: 0-87923-815-1
Library of Congress Catalog Card Number: 89-45390

FIRST EDITION
Printed in the United State of America

Contents

Acknowledgments

Acknowledgment is gratefully made to the following periodicals:

THE AMERICAN POETRY REVIEW: "Late One Night"

BLUE BUILDINGS: "This Letter in Bondage"

GREAT RIVER REVIEW: "Lovesong of the Pale Touch-Me-Not"

GREEN MOUNTAINS REVIEW: "Candles," "Epitaph for a Mosquito Hawk,"
"Four Seasons of His Discontent"

THE JOURNAL: "Inferno"

THE KENYON REVIEW: "Dance of the Mourning Child," "A February Thaw
Should Be Played Slowly," "From the Temple of Longing"

THE LOUISVILLE REVIEW: "The History of the World"

MISSISSIPPI REVIEW: "Fathers and Sons," "The January Thaw"

THE MISSOURI REVIEW: "Florida," "Infant Bonds of Joy," "Children in the Field"

THE NEW REPUBLIC: "Northern Gothic," "Red Cars"

THE NORTH AMERICAN REVIEW: "Father Hunger and Son"

PLOUGHSHARES: "Saturday Morning"

POETRY: "Barn Cat Summer," "The Forever Bird," "For the Reader,""Just
Another Sunset," "Nightwatch," "Persona Non Grata," "Then My
Father's Insomnia Will Break Like The Wine Glass I Crushed
Underfoot At My Wedding"

POETRY EAST: "A Poet's Prayer"

POETRY MISCELLANY: "Lullaby," "A Sentimental Education," "Second
Story," "Surprise Party," "Lovesong of the Spotted Touch-Me-Not"

QUARTERLY WEST: "Night Signals"

THE REAPER: "Your Lips, My Convalescence"

SHENANDOAH: "Lunch at the Russian Tea Room"

"The History of the World" appeared in LIGHT YEAR '85, Bits Press.

"Barn Cat Summer" was reprinted in The Anthology of Magazine
Verse, Monitor Books, 1987.

"A Sentimental Education" was reprinted in Roth's American Poetry Annual, 1989.

Heartfelt thanks to Mark Cox, Ellen Lesser, and Robert Long for
their help in shaping the manuscript; to the Vermont Council on
the Arts; to Norwich University, and the Dana Foundation.

I.

LULLABY

Late One Night

This time around the pale green
light of the moon ignites the restless
underbelly of leaves scraping the window.
A little boy cries out then takes
my nose like a nipple, warm between his teeth
and I could sleep there but the great
calloused palm of the trucker's hand
grinds gears up the interstate,
while the rectum of a dog dozing
at the foot of the bed, like a sculptor
beneath his masterpiece, flutters in the wind
of his devotion. And I welcome your eyelids
with a kiss to the religious
order of insomnia, that gathers and groans in the light
reflected off your dark side hidden
under the quilt I make for, burrow
and nuzzle, belly and thigh, spiraling into the wild
coverthieving configuration. Men's pubic hair
is just a sideshow to the main event, you whisper
and dive back into your dream of judgmental
high-school cronies chained to a tree. Once,
driving the wrong side of a pitch dark
northern highway, seventy-two
cents in the ashtray on a nearly deserted, newly
constructed Sunday night, I swore to the headlights
coming my way, if I could find
an entrance ramp to exit from or a gas pump
in front of a general store about to close,
I swore I'd cross myself with ashes, take vows and mate
with a porcupine. But sometimes, when I don't

know why I'm living or speaking to no one
like you, the feel of that steering wheel falls
into my hands and I drive that right
whale of a car up the ramp like a shiek
whispering into the ear of his camel. And you
can be sure that barrel-shaped
ancient with an accent so thick
it hung in the air like tobacco spit
unlocked his pump for a fairy-tale
handful of change—but then I drove
off the road onto a pier jutting
over a lake that was frozen and waiting
around for the lucky likes
of me, but I had brakes that held and a reverse
gear that brings me back
to you to say that for weekend
after weekend my best friend filled
his pockets from raised tiers of candy bars
wrapped in cellophane and impossible claims
that would fire his tastebuds into Three
Musketeers fighting it out with the Cardinal's
guard or Buck Rogers skyrocketing
the Milky Way. One day
he died in surgery. The next, my first grade
teacher sat me down, crying
or laughing to spite myself,
behind the upright piano, her hand
a battering ram of understanding, pushing
me down into the cobwebbed silence. Then she played
a little something on the dark side
of the keyboard I can't remember.

Candles

We used to steal them
from the general store
and the village church

and smoke ourselves
into an oblivion of screwing
while the ceiling flickered

to the all-night rock 'n' roll.
Before that, there was a night
on that tiny, northern

New England campus when I walked
the snow-blown
path between dorms,

one arm around a book, hands
in my pockets, looking away
from the milky way of candlelit

rooms—a night
that I fell
to my knees in a late

adolescent scream of loneliness,
cried, until breathless
I put my mouth to the path

so cold it burned, and laughed
tossing *The Birth*
of Tragedy into snowfire.

Venereal candlelight
of the next semester: penicillin-
filled syringe burning the other

cheek on the Sabbath, then,
at the beginning of the business
week, two more needles like birthday

candles for a guy who thought
with his prick, my dad would say
any chance he got. Twenty years

of nights into the future, I watched
the reflection of a seven-day
candle mourning a death, a nervous

flame just outside the window,
like the hovering
soul of my father-in-law taken

by surprise but unwilling to leave
his family to their own devices.
At the wake, someone spilled

a day out of the glass cylinder
of milky wax, and while I watched it,
night after night, make the room

quaver, the child on his knees,
afraid and running a fever
inside my body, prayed that Stanley

would stay close by,
that the candle would last forever.
It didn't.

Northern Gothic

... the lives most of us lead — SHAW

There's a rat dead in the crotch
of my son's pajamas, composed
as a Soviet diplomat. His pelt

has a bittersweet
chocolate sheen, well fed
on poisoned wheat, not relevant

to the lives most of us lead
in the suburbs of the beaver
pond without beavers, not listening

to the romance language of deer
droppings falling under a luminous
acid rain, walking

through a scattering of shotgun shells,
red and gold littering the field
like poppies, where the general

practitioner nailed his wife
to a post and beam. Turning
up the volume of his personal stereo,

he jogged to the trailer
of a young, upwardly mobile
neighbor who was setting the table

with plates of irradiated
vegetables and wine, listening
to "All Things Considered" on the radio,

when the doctor stepped in
and turned off the light.

Lullaby

He was watching a movie.
His eyes were closed.
His feet were bloated
raw meat, guilty
of unimaginable crime
against the state, tied
to the legs of a metal chair.
One-third of his mind
was black and blue. One-third
of the world still tortures
anyone left
or right of its opinion,
and when a subtle
turn and technological
twist occurs to a specialist,
it trickles down the torture
grapevine to someone somewhere
who threatens the state
by being no one, his clothes
on a far wall hung on a peg,
like a piñata
suspended in the urinous air
of a dream, beaten
by amused soldiers celebrating
children falling with the clay
shards into space, that corner
of memory where the human
spirit, bolted to the floor,
cannot reach. His wife
in the cell across
from where he sits

in the history of his own
poison was visited
by a stream of figures in white
gowns, sterile masks, and stethoscopes
that rose and fell between her breasts
as she screamed at their leisure
into morning. His eyes were closed.
He was watching a movie
through the busy eye
of a needle sewing remains
of his imagination into a quilt to cover her.
She died.
He never confessed.
They never asked him to.

The January Thaw

She unlaces the blue
leather around her ankle,

kneeling away from the moon-
lit pines, like dancers

in white arm bands, their arms
outstretched and surrounding the lake.

Then something falling startles
the farthest reach of her staring

through the jackknifed upside-down figure
bound hand and foot and tied

to a branch. Veins black
and carved into the gray

flesh of his forearms, muscles
bunched and pulling

away from his spine suspended above
snow-covered shrubs that camouflage

a third party who brushes
frost from his moustache

and crushes the red
glow of a cigarette

between his thumb and forefinger.
The skater's

sweater is a thick, plum-colored
smoke. The crucifix charm

floats on the yarn between her breasts
and the fall of her hair

in the frozen air frames her breath—
while her fingertips over skates

lace them up again. Snow
from pine needles melts down her neck.

A cloud
thin as a jellyfish swallows the moon.

The skater slowly
glides toward the bone-breaking

sound of dogs chasing a deer over dry
winter sticks. The man

with his wrists tied to his ankles,
who wouldn't love her

for all the world among the green-gold
weeds and cold waters, waits

to be released from the thin boundary
between death and desire by the downward

spiral of her skates.

Night Signals

We're in the root cellar overgrown
at the outskirts of the great war

that carried its message across our village.
Most of our neighbors, if they haven't

been cut down or carried off, are bone-tired
and huddled in the runoff

of last night's rain, when Grandmother—the post
and beam of our people, sick

or in need of counsel—climbed up
into the gunpowdered dark to comb what remains

of the rock-swollen, high meadows, avoiding
the level quicksand for an apron

round with leaves and fresh grasses we must
swallow against hunger. Against their parents,

the water-poisoned
children are buckled over and strapped

so they won't drown like Marianka's
little ones those soldiers, stinking of vodka,

threw together like softwood into the quicksand,
and Marianka—no more than a cobweb

half sitting in the water—hasn't budged. A month or so
ago, three soldiers, carousing in her kitchen,

pulled her to the stable. Ivan, her husband, impaled,
only last week—trying to save the children—on the dull

curve of his scythe, woke the village,
who stomped the marauders with anything

they could lay hands on.
I had just calmed the sheep and was threading my way

through moon-shadowed mounds of dirt
and ash—farmers once and where they stood—when I saw

the soldiers being carried off, their eyes
crushed and flowing like red coals, and Grandmother

sweeping the skirmish out of the soil. Through cracks
in the barn boards, watching the dead and harness slide

into the quicksand out of the two-wheel cart, three
bareback riders heading north, and a procession of

women breaking up the dawn, I fell asleep and dreamt
I pushed my herd over the causeway

and never came back, waking
in her strong arms, in this root cellar

I never saw before the war paused like a scythe
in its purposefully easy upside-down arc

coming forward and backward through the pointed air.

Nightwatch

Look at me, said the moon through the spinal
cords of ivy spilling from the hanging pot. I am

the white of bone fractured as you fell
like a four-legged meteor out of a playground

sky—white and sudden as the slap your mother
administered when you were in middle school. I illuminate

the sheet wrapped around the woman's back, the simple rise
of her hip from the lowlands of her waist. She

is a marble sea of serenity
turned away from you—white of the poem

you'd like to carve into the phosphorescence
that won't let you sleep, listening to the tidal

rhythms of your children floating back
and forth between their mother who knows

everything there is to know, and you
wondering when they'll hate you on sight.

Search the moon-shadowed craters of memory
for your father lifting

his suspenders over his shoulders or walking
sideways, like a hermit crab wearing a safe-

deposit box into the next world. Poplar leaves
outside your window rattle and glow. Alert

weariness vibrating under your skin at three A.M.
should tell you we have hours

to reminisce about the missing piece of the stratosphere
or your grandfather's emphysema drifting

with his cigar in neutral off a cliff. I'm happy
if you are just to stay in orbit, turning

with the sleepless likes of you. Look
at the ten moons that rise

in your fingernails, rising beyond the little
moment of your life—these are my

satellite children and I will speak to them
as I speak to you before and after

your departure. Rest in peace.

Then My Father's Insomnia Will Break Like the Wine Glass I Crushed Underfoot at My Wedding

---

I back the red light of my car into the dark
morning and aim the remote control

at my wife in a housecoat recovering
from surgery, waving

happy birthday from the garage, her beehive
hairdo glowing orange between silhouettes

of garbage cans backlit from the inner door,
and press the button. In my headlights

tent caterpillars curl around branches,
chewing leaves like the hungry

souls of my ancestors, nomads once, the first
commuters, ritual butchers, circumcisors

who licked the blood to finish the job, rabbis
who wore their boots to bed waiting

for the messiah—the eyes
of my firstborn everywhere

like predators surrounding this
sleeplessness, circling the back

edge of the pool no longer polluted by a strangely
ungrateful sister or the other

damaged goods of my relations.
In a cruise-controlled

hair over the legal speed—in cool, burgundy
privacy—the sun

over easy in the rear view mirror follows me
across the river you could light a match on

past the shack where men
who work for me swallow dried herrings

like something plucked from the dead—
the smell of that

follows me over industrial flats, shadowed
by mounds of slag and sulphur, beneath the great

prehistoric gut belching orange
flame into black cloud. Tomorrow,

Pearl Harbor Day, my Daughter
of the American Revolution secretary will rail against

the foreign invaders. The next, the Feast
of the Immaculate Conception, is the birthday

of my son, that embarrassment who left his wife
for someone he never bothered to introduce me to.

And when
this firstborn pariah calls

he'll say, "You're sixty-six," and pay his respects.
And I'll pay mine and mention other

calls waiting, who needs
the aggravation, maybe next year he won't bother

and I can close my eyes like a somnambulist
who can waltz backward

into any bank in town, borrow a million
on his signature—a religious man who smuggles

Jews out of the asshole of communism and pays
right through the nose for every

peaceful moment, every sweet
second of revenge on half the nightmare

of my life: the relentless need
of my first wife, and the cancer, random

and blistering under the skin of the second
while I hold my breath.

Father Hunger and Son

A pedestal ashtray next to the son who hadn't seen
or spoken to his father for years of blame, and another
man wrapped in a coat, both hands pressed
into a fist between his thighs, the cleanshaven
pendulum of his chin muttering under a petrified
tear that magnified the bloodshot corner. Jealous
of his thirty years side-by-side with my father
working the phones for sales, I assumed his grief
was for the tenuous life at the far end
of the corridor suspended between
a bag of blood and a monitor's
vigilance. I touched his shoulder like a stranger
interrupting another on an empty bus. He'll be okay.
Who? he answered, as he grabbed
the ashtray and pulled it to him, whispering
through something stuck in his throat
that he'd found an unmailed
letter from his wife to another man
sticking out from under
the car seat as he'd reached to turn the key
that morning in the garage. I want him to masturbate
to death, he said. You can see
your father now, the nurse told me.
After I passed my stepsister and Aunt Delilah, her eyebrows
raised into dollar signs beneath a pale
beehive, my stepmother pulled me aside and said,
Why are you here? You're not welcome. You'll kill him
if you step foot in that room. I pushed
my sad cuckold into a cab that dropped us
in the industrial flats under cranes looming
by the revolving bridge of my childhood

over the river that burned once. While we tried
to light it again with matchbooks and wads
of old receipts from his pockets, scraps
of smoke drifting nowhere, he wanted to know
what I thought he should say to his wife. I asked him
if my father loved me. He hunkered down
and stared at his wingtips. When your mother
left him for that other guy, something
died inside of him. I'm not saying he didn't laugh
or give a shit about anyone. But if
your name came up—which was almost
never—you could see something
sidestep in his face, like he was dodging
a sucker punch. What do I know after thirty years
of lunches and hustle? I worked for the bastard.
He signed the checks like clockwork every week.
As I started to cry, he said, C'mere, child,
crying too and pulling me
to his sandpaper cheek. I don't know my wife
any better than your old man. Or anyone else
for that matter. I don't know.

II.

FOUR SEASONS OF HIS DISCONTENT

Epitaph for a Mosquito Hawk

Your wife on her knees by moonlight
searched the weeds for a bottle
flung from a window or a pan of beer

to share with slugs, gray and floating
face down. Like Bonaparte
the village clown, your face

was the bloated emperor
of bullfrogs perched on the short loaf
of your brave white body that insisted

everyone in town for the annual
anticommunist Christian revival
listen hard to your every

utterance of divinely expiring
gospel, look upon your spotlighted
radiance, and worry

about seeking your favor, so year
after year they could return
to get even closer to the inner

circle of the crucifixion in the next round
of musical prayers. Younger women
in the choir, enrobed in crimson and ivory,

like mosquitos, blood-swollen and captured
in a jar, were delicacies you gnawed on
to assuage your spiritual hunger, spitting

the remains into the garden, where your wife
on her knees by moonlight
combed the weeds for a kidney

to have with her beer. And though
this epitaph is a touch premature, let
me say that it came in a vision

of starvation devouring every word
you've ever written and that
I wrote it down to cheer you

and clear the air of heathen
anarchist-vegetarian
detractors, you would say, so the next world

will better smell the forthcoming sweet
exhalation of your soul—may these
meditations lubricate

your original path to an early
reservation in the private
dining room of the holy

of holies in the night café. Children,
I'm turning my back and bending
over the untarnished dearly departed Christian

soldier's memory, who cut
one deadly pinko viper
after another from the rotting

plaque in the gums of humanity, and lifting
my arms in benediction over his
untimely demise. And may that light substance,

winged and sacred, pass
like an eternal baptism over his soul. Glory
to a world fragile as the buzz

of an insect in the hearing aid of a paranoid
spiritual leader about to depart
with the tin ear of a wounded

war hero and a Purple Heart. Halleluyah.
God is love. Say it.

Four Seasons of His Discontent

I've been digging a hole in sunlight.
I've been running uphill
on a sheet of ice. I've taken

my innermost being by the collar
and hurled it at the first
hawk of spring gliding

above its furry breakfast. You can bet
that I wanted to make
the right impression on a cluster fly

thrashing in the window, that I yearned
even more to have the Bureau of Motivation
inspect every cobwebbed corner

of my self-respect. One moonlit morning,
as I slept in a mud hole in front of my shack,
a yellow butterfly landed on peach fuzz

above my lip, whispering into the two-way
tunnel of my slumbering nose, "Hey Weingarten
of The Lake, I'm the reincarnation

of your Uncle Hyman and I'll fricassee
your *tuchas* with a Bunsen burner
if you don't cut the crap." I wanted to wake

from that beauty sleep and pull
the sword out of the stone of my
sickness unto death; I wanted to climb the bald

mountain of my anxiety, turn my shoulder
blades of resentment into wings flying
out of the quicksand of my self-contempt. Instead

I've been tunneling away at daylight, trying to defy
gravity up an icy hill. Stopped a man of the cloth
in his car, who took one look, crossed himself

and ran the light. Reader, though I haven't
resolved a damn thing, I promise not
to let you down: My dentist said nowadays

it's hard to find a good hygienist, but you
can find me almost anytime with a half-eaten
pickled egg in one hand and a warped

cue over my shoulder, pacing
around the table at the Miss Montpelier
Tap and Grill. Remember the schoolboy

who overheard a cockroach telling God
on the ceiling of the Sistine Chapel
that becoming was superior to being, and who

can argue that? So slide your quarter
into the slot and rack 'em tight,
so the black ball you've been waiting for

lingers, while the rest explode. House
rules. Winner breaks,
but I'll leave you a shot.

For the Reader

Under the smoke and ice-covered roof, next
to the nickel-plated parlor stove, there sat,

in an easy chair, an old friend, who would not
speak or move to greet me, whose eyes

were wide and riveted to
Bachelard's *The Poetics of Space.* After work,

the next day, I returned with a valentine;
my old friend, still in the chair,

staring. I raised two fingers
to the lids of nearly

nicotine-yellow and bloodshot eyes, and noticed,
out of the corner of mine, the distraction

of a jay gliding between the evening
sun and the bay window, shadowing, for less

than a moment, the first line of the first page
of Bachelard's *The Poetics of Space.*

Lunch at the Russian Tea Room

My mouth reflected in the glass
over my smiling war-hero brother's

last photograph can taste the shredded
fiction of my soul sliding down

into the zippered side-compartment
of my purse. Trained in Odessa

by a practitioner of the art
of sudden reversals, I learned the KGB

holy trinity: how to hold
your breath for minutes; how to stop

your heart; and how to vomit at will—
a distraction which,

as a specialist for a prestigious
international firm,

I've called upon before a captive
audience of an overly

curious colleague, a client
in heat, and a representative

of an unspecified government. Here,
in the splendor of an indecent meal,

I can laugh under my breath and say
if it weren't for gravity, I could turn

the gilded ceiling into a roiling sea
of Renaissance anatomies, part the waters,

and while everyone's scrambling
to get ashore, slide an ice pick

through the ear of my double-dealing
silent partner across the table. After

each long and leisurely course of blini,
borscht, or delicate piroshke,

I can taste my past—backstroking
the rape meadow outside Moscow, swimming

against the tide with the love
of my life, climbing out of the oily

stalks, yellower than my mother's
nicotine fingernails chewed

to the quick—as I release it forever
into my oversized purse. After that,

I'll hold my breath for an easy
two minutes, stop my heart, and reach,

like a duck hunter searching
marshy waters for his kill,

for the loaded
little present I promised myself

for dessert.

Fathers and Sons

I've been reading lately about a bloodhound-
faced old buzzard who had a yen for bartering
whole countries of illiterate poor, who felt

right at home posing with a general in macho
mirrored sunglasses and an everlasting frown,
the gold-braided uniform filling the photograph

like a false pregnancy. When the general's
close relations felt like moving in
on the old man's estates and mistresses,

he caught wind of it, and threw a dinner
for all concerned, all of whom died
toasting the general, who didn't, so the old man asked

if he would care to join him on the porch swing
for brandy and a good cigar. Like little boys delirious
with kidding each other, they caroused

until the old man started breathing
evenly on the general's shoulder, who thought he might cook
the old fellow's brains in black butter for breakfast,

but, as he was quietly unsheathing his sword,
a woman in a mask stepped out of the shrubbery
with a small weapon and a glass and invited him to drink.

As the general tilted the pale
yellow liquid to his thin lips, the old man
shot the assassin between the eyes. The general swore

he loved the old man like a father, who swore
he loved the general like a lost child returned
after many years. They kissed each other, embraced

and cried, cursing their enemies, when another
junta swooped down and buried them
alive under the porch, like an old husband

and his new bride.

The History of the World

Believing the soul resides in the nose, a fourteenth-
century wife of a Castillian aristocrat, having learned
her husband was going to guillotine her nose
as a wedding present for her successor, stuffed it

with holy water, myrrh, and a wad of honeycomb.
A nose at birth begins to die and the end begins
at the beginning. The imperfect shadow of a stuffed
nose is the new poetic. A partial eclipse of the

moustache, and Wilhelm Reich climbs a fever, giving
birth to a phenomenology of the nose that understands
what's written on the wind of the right nostril
is engraved in the ring around the left. He stuffs his

with a mixture of fermented shark's meat and illuminated
scrolls that depict St. Joseph riding a tortoise
around the recumbent Virgin submerged
in a goblet of steam glazing her Wedgewood

nostrils. . . . In San Francisco, handkerchiefs
travel under the counter at the speed of light.
A nun, lowering the drawbridge for a priest, wore a
black handkerchief over her face for thirty years that

lifted in the wind of her devotions. There's ectoplasm
in the air. You can't xerox
a stuffed nose leaping from a Lady Godiva
chocolate-covered peach to a bowl of gelatinous

red and yellow antihistamines. Raiders
of a nose-shaped pyramid of the Upper Nile
opened a delicatessen on the Lower East Side.
In Los Angeles, unemployed

dairy farmers injected silicone into the clear
passages of go-go dancers until both nostrils filled
to Renaissance proportions. As the golden trumpet
of the herald bloomed in the stratosphere,

the imperfect shadow of a horn of plenty was set
in heaven and sat on a throne. Doc Holiday
and Wyatt Earp filled theirs with lead balls,
black powder, and spun the chambers. If the eye

of the nose interecedes for the rectum,
can the state of repose achieved by Erasmus,
fallen from his mount with kidney stones in 1506,
be far behind? In Palm Beach, a full nostril's

looked upon as a sign of breeding. Speaking
from the nose is regarded as more etheric,
godlike. . . . Another poet, believing his nose
was haunted by W. H. Auden and Jesus Christ,

relied on an Ouija board to speak for the spirits.
Black market transistorized nose hair cutters
laundered off the Florida coast are highly prized
by libertines and vegetarians tumbling

out of one nose into another. Queen Victoria
negotiated a liquor license for the Prince of Wales'
nose, the swinging doors of his nostrils opening
into the twentieth century, where Frank

Lloyd Wright was waiting to model the first skyscraper
after a Q-tip. An old man with three nostrils
and a bad cold is looked upon with no little reverence
in the back rooms of the Kremlin. How sweet the aroma

rising from the appetite of one who wished
Weingarten's nose was filled with nickels. Whither
the years and who can remember. O sinusitis, mingling
with love and poetry, lead the way through ivy-covered

Stations of the Cross into the inner sanctum
of the eardrum, where I may live out my life, holding
up the cocoon of my nose to the inner light,
like a glass paperweight to a window, watching

the wings of my godlike self, my hermit
almost ready to fly. My stuffed nose I do bequeath
to our great brother Villon and to earth our mother
I bequeath a tincture of goldenseal and the common cold.

Nicolai Vasilievich Gogol drop-kicked a nose
baked in a piroshke and wearing a uniform
down Nevsky Prospect, swearing under his breath
that a stuffed nose can live twenty-seven thousand

days without a hankie, but a clean handkerchief
will die of heartbreak in a dark pocket.

This Letter in Bondage

...and there was none that could deliver the ram out of his hand.
—8:7. THE BOOK OF DANIEL

This letter mailed to you for luck came to life
in a leather pouch—over which the Postmaster Of Us All,
near and far, inclined his ear—nestled in the foothills
of Southern Arkansas. And having sailed around
the worldly sphere, like a night crawler
stowed away in the belly of a satellite, the luck

has passed to you. Wherefore the she goat
waxed large, and you, providing you put this letter
in orbit, will conceive good luck in four days
and a vision of cracked pottery in the eerie
dusk of the winds of heaven raising up and down
the bloodstains on her skirts; therefore, you'll come

down from the windowsill wonderfully. Send
twenty copies, no cash, to the Goodwill
handicapped, and they will be identical and multiply.
The wild ewe of fate has no price, no head. If
you hoard this letter around after hours, you might
be smothered, suddenly, like the Roman Lucretia

by the son of Tarquin's kisses. Selah!
A Parisian cheese-maker, embracing
a vision of whey in an ecstasy and some big
profits that weighed on her conscience, buried
this letter under an ancestral footstone on a slope,
losing her step to an epidemic

of the inner ear. Admiral Footy's psychic mother,
knitting in a wheel chair, raised a hue, a cry,
a swoon, and died because he failed to circulate
his luck through this prayer in bondage. Before this,
a round sum of gold bullion appeared on the horizon.
Before he drowned, a cable arrived that swore,

up and down, that his mistress had her way
with a leper. Hail Mary. It works. Send it
to twenty convicts and see their luck change.
This luck is bound to come to you even if
you are not a fundamentalist. Try it on your parents—ere
this prayer is through you will note the following:

here, in Norway, Olafson, the king's veterinarian,
was fooling around with a wolfhound
when he received this chain. She bit the tip
of his flat blue nose. He grabbed for it but not
before she swallowed it in a way that made him faint.
He rose up and did the king's business on the hill.

The next day he was sacked but found an even better
position lugging crazed Norwegian cormorants
in a bucket I can still hear crying in the bluffs
around the periphery of this letter in bondage.
Remember, this is no joke. I can vouch for it.
Now away with you. P. S. Bjorntregger, an "automobile"

Amishman, a famed seeker of land uncluttered
by the anxiety of architecture and fast trains,
who called himself *The Strange One*, was leaving
the suburbs of St. Louis for the unrolling
prairie of Weingarten—have faith
or check your atlas—when he collided

with a miracle of horses towing a Budweiser
beer wagon. Losing their heads to the black hood
of his three-quarter-ton camper special, two
great yellow manes twirling blood
and harness—like the twin fire wheels
that tall ship sailors swear on their mothers

bring them luck—reared back just
as their muzzles pressed the windshield
in the slowest motion Bjorntregger will ever
see or be a part of, as if
they were groomed for only that moment, one
coming down on the brushed gabardine

of his Sunday best; the other, its brother, its
wet nostrils flared with fragments of glass,
falling upon an ancient postmark becoming even redder
in the polished, pitch-black, Naugahyde
crevice of the passenger seat. The wagon driver
was lucky. Need I say more?

Florida

The tail end of the hurricane
into the outskirts of Orlando: waves

pressed the road from both sides
and a woman impaled on a branch

of sunlight rode the top of a Volkswagen
bus floating on a lake where the pavement

curved toward Bill's parents' house.
I hadn't slept for two days. Cigarettes

and hard-selling radio preachers
helped me swerve around an armadillo,

kept me awake. When I got there,
he threw his duffle bag into the boot

and said, I can't take it
anymore. When I woke

looking up at a gas jockey
snapping gum and grinning

through the windshield at my rolled
and tufted face, Bill was confiding

to the animal in the center
of the steering wheel that he found

his mother beating off on the toilet,
her light-blue bathrobe folded twice

on the floor. Then you, he went on,
in your red miracle of a Chevrolet,

sailed in on the warm end of the storm.
And where did that get us?

Almost Virginia, replied the attendant, leaning
an elbow into the window.

That'll be four dollars on the nose.
We watched him grab

a front bumper and swing
into the dark underbelly of the car, waving a

finger knowing we couldn't help
but admire his confidence and grace. Bill said

when he'd been a drummer for the school jazz band
he could play the solo from "Caravan"

until they were climbing the bleachers—style
like that doesn't live forever.

He opened the door, crossed the road
and started hitchhiking back to Florida.

I pulled a U-turn in front of a school bus.
The driver honked. Bill got in,

smiled, and said to the rear view mirror, You don't
have to do this. But you forgot

your duffle. He didn't laugh
at that one. I didn't care, but I wondered

what it felt like to have a family
so sharp in your gut that it could pin you

in the air like a butterfly, pale green
and fragile under glass.

Inferno

"...waves and the sort of smile you cut into your face at times like that."
—ANDRE DUBUS

I'm on a sunset sail between Cuba
and nuclear warheads aimed

in that direction from the tin-roofed
Key West naval base. An anorexic New

Zealand opera singer with a barracuda
smile, who relishes the sight of leaping porpoises

off the starboard bow, shows anyone milling around
where she holds her ground, her ex-husband's pencil

on onionskin refusal to wire
alimony to the states. *No comprendo,* says the semi-

bald man with crucifix earrings, a runny nose and a video
camera sneezing at the all-

female crew who raise sails, tighten ropes
and lower them over and over. A cobra

of smoke wanders out of the corner
of the captain's mouth, reminiscing about late

eighteenth-century pirate booty—emeralds
and gold chain as long as whale penis, and cocaine

you can chase with a margarita
almost anyplace. His chin whiskers lean

into his knuckles, his elbows into a side rail,
proud of his steel-hulled

four-masted schooner, on the lookout for others—
restless and running their engines—that he

would run for their money if he could squeeze
a steady wind out of a fart on a lazy night. I'm

daydreaming of a poster of Dennis Hopper holding
the top of a steering wheel and a cigarette

in his right hand, and a tape recorder
to his cheek, while Bruno Ganz in a bomber jacket

leans his elbow into the roof
over the cleft brim of Hopper's hat, the neon porno-

palace German night in the background. Bruno stares
under his bandaged eyebrow at his life standing still

and reeling out of his grasp, while Hopper's face
is an old leather binding of light and pain

listening to his own voice, remembering an endless
procession of Polaroids of himself aiming the camera at himself

aiming the camera.
A woman in the stern suddenly

screaming about counterrevolutionary
schemes in Nicaragua and the Philippines

slaps her husband, who spanks his daughter, who throws
her doll at the bloodshot sun, setting the world on fire.

III.

INFANT BONDS OF JOY

Children in the Field

I was on my back in a blizzard
of milkweed down the children were flinging
into the wind gusting like geese suddenly
changing direction. The silks caught
in my beard reminded me of a scarf
over my face, leggings, and boots that buckled
over my shoes—it was almost a mile
through snow to my waist on my way
to Mrs. Miller's first grade extravaganza
of Ali Baba, air raid sirens richocheting
off the basement walls at our heads tucked
between our knees, and fingerpainted lightning
taped to the back of the upright piano,
when a blue dot grew into Jake the cop
standing over me in the no man's land
of the five-way intersection, who said I knew
you'd show up. He ducked a snowball
that came out of nowhere and said I'm sorry
about your friend. He was a good kid.
I cupped my hands to my scarf and to the red ear
under the gold-rimmed cap, shouting
that Mike wasn't afraid of germs or bugs.
He ate candy off the street, and almost
destroyed his bully of an older brother
with a fish hook tied to an arrow.
Jake took a swipe
at my tears with his mitten, then turned me
around in the drift, blindfolded
by the white blur, like it was my turn
to pin the tail on the donkey, and wished me
luck as he pushed me back into the blizzard

of children trying to bury me alive under armloads
of leaves. I wheeled around
a corridor of men staring at the ceiling, catheters
dangling off the side of their beds, then returned
to eighth-grade Biology, where my girlfriend
was dissecting the lungs and heart
of a frog pulsing between the curtains
of its skin, pulled back and pinned
to a piece of cardboard. She passed me a formaldehyde-
scented note under the table: Please don't
poke fun at Hyman Lipschitz's
acne anymore. We're going steady. I looked up
at the bold letter of his name engraved
on the bracelet swaying from her wrist
as she performed a last incision with her eyes
closed because she didn't want to see
the hash she was making
or me whispering maybe
we could jitterbug at his bar mitzvah.
Leaning closer to steal
a last kiss, I gagged at the smell
between us and threw up with several
others close by following suit. She crawled
toward the door, while Mr. Schwartz
pulled me by my hair wrapped around his knuckles
to the blackboard, bounced my head
against it, screaming Filth
and Nincompoop, then he told me
I had four minutes to clean it up. This
was Painesville, where my sister never smiled
or stepped outside our father's house, the richest
farm between Erie and Sandusky, our closest neighbor
a thief everyone called
Reuben the Stick, because he chewed
twigs and spat the bark wherever he pleased, or Reuben
the Conqueror because he'd never been caught. Once,

my father on a ladder was finishing
a pyramid of silver dollars. I interrupted the sun
setting on his masterpiece to read him a letter
from Reuben, who praised my sister's
inner beauty and demanded thirty thousand
for a dowry or else he'd take an axe
to our vineyards and bleed
our prize Nubians with his own teeth.
Please inform Mr. Reuben Mintz, said my father,
that he may kiss my tuchas,
then lifted his slipper to the next
to the hightest rung. Men with guns
answered my knock and brought me
to an easy chair across from Reuben
the Conqueror, who offered me wine and a word
about my future prospects in his firm.
Barefoot, I entered my sister's room. She snored
into her pillow, a string of drool
trailing off under the quilt. I shook her,
whispering that she should prepare
a feast fit for an emperor and herself
with ointments and a crown of miniature
roses in her hair. Delighted
with the powdered cinnamon
scattered over the pigeon pie, my father pretended
not to notice the extra chair or the trace
of a smile on my sister's lips when he stood
to answer the tattoo
rapped on the door with a gun butt.
Two of Reuben's sidekicks said
Come with us. We've prepared a little surprise
before supper. Behind the five-story barn,
on a rise, kerosene-light flickered
over my grandparents' headstones—a fresh
grave between them glowed like a lava flow
and they lowered my father to Reuben waiting

with a lantern and a knife.
A big wedding or a small funeral, it's up to you,
said the Stick. You're very considerate, said my father,
who took a pistol like a handkerchief
from his dinner jacket, shooting Reuben
in the leg and his henchmen above, who joined
negotiations in the open grave. Like a shooting
star in reverse, my father sailed the knife
into the night, then climbed the stack
of bodies after it, calling me
and my sister in tears to welcome
Reuben to the family. Five thousand,
said my father to the Conqueror,
or I'll let you bleed. Unable to breathe, I burst
with the snarl of a wild cat through the burial
mound of leaves and children, scaring them
all the way to the house, where they beat me
with pillows until I confessed
I was a monkey's uncle, but that
was another story of a wounded soldier disguised
as a wild beast, traveling at the edge
of enemy territory in the rain,
when all of sudden a fire seemed
to spring out of the crotch of a shagbark
hickory at the side of the road, and they twisted
my arm until I told it.

The Forever Bird

When you and I were children we wondered
what it would be like to burn

someone at the stake. We gathered
the makings of a good fire and drove

a broom handle into the rotting
sweetness of the woods at the bottom

of our street, where we went
almost every day to bury

little boys' treasure, catch a monarch
or carve acorns into faces

that talked back to us
in a language only we could hear.

On the way to find the new kid
I realized what would happen

if we went ahead with it.
I had left you with hard candy

and a wooden match, listening to the clear
endless song of a bird we called

the forever bird, invisible
in the high branches of the highest tree.

You sat, drawing in the dirt with a twig,
until a thrashing in the leaves scared you

all the way up the street, where you found me
at the attic window, on the lookout for smoke

rising through the treetops, imagining
you giving up on me and burning

the orange cat that followed us
to our hiding place. Your face was blue;

your lips, purple. In a few weeks,
your operation would go awry. In my dream

a forearm pushes up like a weed
through your front yard, the fist

opening into a blanket, which I peel back
to reveal your old man's face

whistling the forever song. Then your mother,
coming across the lawn, tells me

you're on the roof with a fever—
Come back tomorrow.

Second Story

Those days
I stayed up later than my brother, who levitated
his covers with an endless reservoir
of farts and groans, while I waited at the window for the mystery
to reveal itself, listening to "Cool it Baby" or "Don't
Knock the Rock" on the radio. Cynthia and her sister's bedroom
window shade across from ours was pulled
almost all the way down. Summer lightning
burned the sky, frost like a jungle climbed the glass,
and a softball-sized hailstone rolled off Cynthia
and her sister's roof in April. Older kids, behind her house,
teased us until Cynthia cried, or pinned us
on roots sloping away from the backyard oak.
So we played in the sideyard, a gate at one end, an ivy-
covered trellis at the other. One day, while we were plotting
to free the world of those bullies—pouring
liquids scrounged from the broom closet and cellar
back and forth between bottles we buried
under a shrub—I told her how I stayed up, looking
out the window facing hers, that I had seen a pale
February moon pause for a second on her chimney,
while the neighbors across the street, drunk
and screaming out of their car, went still until it passed
behind a cloud. We looked at each other in a spell
her mother broke. That night the bedroom shade
was pulled almost all the way down over the yellow rectangle
of light that filled the room around a mirage of upper thigh
to belly as the undergarment I had no name for
slipped off into nowhere and a nightshirt fell
over the triangle of hair. But when Cynthia or her sister's

hand reached like an electric charge for the shade, to open
or close it, I knocked the radio off the night table
and my brother out of his dreamless drifting into adolescence,
diving in a fever through my confusion, where I stayed
until sunrise.

Saturday Morning

for Michael Trombley

Single file out of Hebrew
history class in bow ties
and jackets, skull caps
and double-knotted shoes. I didn't want
to sit for hours and pray
to a foreigner in a foreign tongue.
I wanted to cross the street
to the elevator, opening
on the Viola Gensler
School of Ballet, the perspiring
glass door. I pretended
to tie my shoe and let the boys
behind me veer and pass
like carpenter ants into the great
turquoise-and-gold dome. I climbed
a ladder, pushed through the roof,
and rode the unfolding
fire escape into freedom. The elevator
doors parted, and she
was waiting: black tights
and soiled, pink canoes
with bows tied around the ankles.
The red mirage
smeared her cheeks and the dark
cobalt shadow stared me down
to the first floor. I turned
the handle at the aquarium shop.
The bell rang. The old man
looked up over gold-rimmed
spectacles and said, "Keep your fingernails

off the glass, you'll kill the fish.
It will cost you." At the end
of the aisle, I came face-to-face
with the orange piranha. The rotting
picket fence of the old man's teeth
said, "All you little Jewboys
stop there, don't you?" before he ducked
behind his paper. A bubble of air
rose to the surface. The fish stared
while I bashed my forehead
into the glass. There was no pain. Only
the old man drowning
me in curses and spit. The fish stared.

A Sentimental Education

The arm out of nowhere, the fall
from my bike—the spitting
voice, the fist: kike
over and over—the hypnotic
eyes under a cropped
wheat field of hair, looking down
at me wondering
what I had done: this boy
hating me on sight, a wild
name on his lips like a flying
leap up a mountain with tail
and ball of string attached.

I loved the sound of her bra
snapping in fifth grade. I held
my breath when she ran
up the aisle of gentile
children laughing despite
the blue-wigged teacher scolding
until my friend stepped
back into the light
rain of silence, her new shoes
creaking on the linoleum. We held

hands in the last row of a choral
platoon of bow ties—red and green—
and tinsel. We refused
to sing Jesus or Mary,
substituting Yiddish
like *tuchas* and *schmooz*. Someone
reported us and we had to fill

blackboards around the room, the chalk
screeching Holy Jesus until sunset.
One morning the teacher drove
right through the long pole and flag
I held over the crosswalk. Out of the yellow

hood of my slicker, I yelled
You crazy son of a bitch. She rolled
her window down to say that none
of you Jewish kids have any couth, the rain
driving her rouge into the ancient
wrinkle. The whole class, except my friend
and a boy named Walter, voted to banish
me from Safety Patrol. I tried
not to cry as I gave them a one-
finger salute passing through the cloakroom
toward Miss Van Deusan's office, but the teacher
sent another boy to bring me back. He grabbed

my wrist in the hall and I punched him
in the breadbasket, then his nose
bled and he beat me
to the principal, who lectured us
on leadership, restraint, and spy
satellites circling the earth,
her tight red hair
raised into a torch
over the pink shells of her ears
that could hear the ocean.

Infant Bonds of Joy

In the chrome mouth of the Edsel
I straightened my bow tie as my uncle
pulled a long, clay-green
cigar from a metal tube. He spat
the tip at a ginkgo. He quoted Flaubert,

who, after he was cured of syphilis
in the French mud and marked for life
with black saliva, said, "I
am like a cigar: you have to suck on the end
to get me going." My father, embarrassed,

brought a match to my uncle's
cleft chin as my brother and I
walked inside the lazy
afternoon at my grandparents that began
its slow descent peeling galoshes

and scarves, feeling the brittle
bones of my grandfather's fingers
pushing us toward the red-winged
crashing against the wicker cage. "What's
the white stuff in bird doo?"

he whispered. "Tell me and I'll fly you
to Miami Beach." My mother,
lifting the foil from a black cake,
wadded it into a ball and threw it hard
at my father, knocking his hat into a bowl

of chopped liver and schmaltz across the room
where my brother was crawling
under the table with a cousin to spy
on Grandmother's tears sliding
into her moustache and dripping into the great

cleavage as she grated horseradish into the bowl
of beet juice. "What an awful thing
life is," said that same Frenchman, who lived at home
with his mother, "like soup with a hair floating on top
you have to eat it nevertheless." Two years

like back-to-back slow dances at a bar mitzvah,
then the children were told to stay in the car,
the engine running
to keep us warm, gray
snow building a wall over the windshield. I drew

stick figures across the tinted glass, while my uncle's
soul, ready to leap, stared
from his coffin at the six-pointed star.
When my grandfather died in my uncle's arms
the year before, his last words

were indistinguishable from the cry
of his red bird through the swinging
door of the kitchen where my brother and I
in a fever were tasting whiskey
from everyone's glass. From that

childhood to running
naked through a blizzard: an attempted
teenage suicide that left me
feeling better than skipping the perfect stone
of self-hate out of my body, hovering awhile

on the surface and whistling "Flat Foot
Floojie with a Floy Floy." A convoy
of Roger Midwest tractor-trailers will run
over and over the unleavened bones
of my being in limbo between

remembered joy and the fumes and sulphur haze
of adulthood. Flattened
into a roadside marker, I will point the way.
My plaque will say Weingarten
never really lived, but

when he does appear in the dashboard
glow of your imagination, traveler,
strike your match against his epitaph
and cup your hands to the fire so you
can hold his spirit, yellow and dancing

around a black stick, then be on your way.

Red Cars

The driver's door of the '57 Ford coupe
caught in the snow and bent backwards
as he backed down the driveway on his way
to the middle of his junior year. December child,
he parallel-parked for the inspector
into a drift, while I watched him almost
pass the test. My father found the olive-green
and rusting hulk, covered the seats in barber-pole-
striped vinyl, reamed the engine for my brother's
initiation into the mysteries
of transporting himself, and lacquered
the finish into a maraschino
chariot, like the fire chief's, who unleashed
his siren as my brother laid rubber
at the light. Waiting for me to finish
my toast and cocoa, he bent the door back
in a snow bank. Tensed, like a loaded crossbow,
when I leaned into the window to ask if he
could wait a minute, he let the door
answer my question. Twenty-six
years later, I called to talk about
the business of old jalopies, catering
rock concerts, and selling occasional freight cars
of small appliances. The double carburetor
of his '66 Volvo two-door coupe, he told me,
is like twin bladders: one squirts
all over the snow, while the other
closes up for winter. Come visit
and we'll make them tango. Maybe,
I answered, and went on to resurrect the time
he drove my go-kart into a wall. It's funny

now, I said, but that steering wheel
jammed between your legs drove the sunburn
right out of your face. Between goodbyes
and waiting in silence for the other
to click off, a battle we sometimes fought
for the fun of it after a conversation
went down reasonably smooth, I whispered
Don't sell the Volvo.

Surprise Party

I decided to turn Halloween
inside-out—shave my beard

after twenty years of sheltering
infestations of peanut butter

and sprouts like cabbage worms.
I wanted to know if laughter,

grief, or what's in between
traveled any further than the whiskery

periphery. I wanted to see
if my father's indifference,

my ex-wife's affair, and that
letter from Internal Revenue

had somehow impressed themselves
on the flesh concealed

under the mask of black hair. My co-
conspirators distracted the children

scooping seeds and orange meat, impatient
for the jack-o'-lantern to come to life,

draping the room with spider webs,
bats, and dancing skeletons,

while I scraped and suppressed
the bleeding with thumb and toilet paper.

Neither the horror show I feared
nor the twenty-one-year-old I hoped

to resurrect, I stared into the reflection,
thinking I looked too much like my father

to be able to stand it. When I materialized
in the kitchen, everyone peeked

between their fingers, hooted and screamed
at the pale-faced old skin. The little one

laughed, the dog flinched, and the eldest
ran to his room, headfirst

under the covers. I ran
after him and put my hand on the rise

of his shoulder blade. He pulled away
with a muffled, How can you do this?

What if I get lost? I won't
be able to find you. Later,

after all of us in sheets played hide-
and-seek with arrows through our heads

and protruding blood-red teeth, he apologized
and even kissed me when I tucked him in.

I'm getting used to it, I heard him whisper
in the dark, as if it were years later

and he was trying to convince
the familiar stranger in his own mirror

that he was welcome.

Dance of the Mourning Child

He opened the door to the kindergarten:
hung his coat on a peg, unbuckled
his boots, and rocked awhile

on his heels. He rifled books
for the porcupine whose only friends
were an opossum with a broken tail

and a nearsighted skunk who treated them
like they were her offspring. He scooped sand
from a pail into a truck. He pulled

his lunch box out of his cubby and nibbled
a sandwich and celery sticks. He woke
in his usual sweat from a nap,

then walked his story
about Princess Badroulboodour, the apple
of Aladdin's eye, all the way home

to my lap. I asked if Neil
used bad words again. He said no,
he wasn't there, but anyway his

mom and dad say it's OK. Where
were the other children? No one
was there and Mrs. Nobody

wasn't there either. That's how it feels
when somebody dies, I said. He rammed
his face into mine. We both

saw stars. When he stopped crying and wiped
his nose on my sleeve, I asked if he wanted
to split a doughnut. I'm thirsty,

he answered. Can we build
the biggest snowman or read about the boy
and his juggling dog that ran away? No

to the snowman; yes to the book. Then he ran
his fist up and down my knee,
making sounds like a race car getting ready.

Tall Wading Birds, India Rubber Men

On my shoulders making fingerprints
on the ceiling, Jonah wanted to know
where to find a real giant. His brother
found one in a book of wonders, who died balancing
a beer keg on his forehead. Climbing down
into my lap, he watched a contortionist on TV bend
over backward, sweep her head
forward between her legs, pick up a glass
of wine in her teeth, and drink it all
without spilling. To meet
this challenge, he arched and dropped,
over and over again into nightfall,
when I recited "The Human Pretzel
of Ranchipur" to ease
the determination in his eyes
into sleep, curled up
with his stuffed menagerie. In the morning
his brother put a hand over my mouth
and a finger to his own. And we tiptoed
downstairs to find him on the porch, throwing one
steak knife after another at my old poster
of Rhonda Fleming he taped to the screen door. I took
the deepest breath I can muster and remembered
drilling the knots out of my father's
pine bar in the basement and how he whaled
the tar out of my overalls, but I still
had the mischief in my heart. I pulled the knives
from the door and handed one to each of my
sideshow daredevils in pajamas
and we kept at it until the screen
disintegrated.

From the Temple of Longing

The moment the children climb
into my ex-wife's car they buckle
themselves into a faraway look.
The little one
never cries, the eldest
counts white hairs that sneak
like the future up the side of his arm.
Camel, tent, oasis, storm—their ancestors
longed to pause and longed even more
to press on. But on a cobalt dark
night like this, following
an invisible need at the other
end of a leash, I want to hear
from my wild nomads dreaming
on the other side of the state. I want
to hear them say, Papa, it's alright,
don't cry—always thirsty at three A.M.
for something more than water. Maybe
you think this is all about a dime-
a-dozen emotional flotsam who left a furious
marriage only to miss his children from one
school holiday to the next, who exaggerates
the tangled heartworms that pressed
his rib cage when his
parents divorced. Maybe you just
want to tell me that children
are not that fragile. But I wonder
what I would hear, a dozen
years from now, waiting for the last
solar eclipse of the century, my arms relaxed
around my teenage boys, hovering

over a jerryrigged
cardboard theater, watching
the little moon erase the little sun—
I wonder what they would say
in that strange light, if I asked them
to remember.

IV.

LOVESONG OF THE PALE
TOUCH-ME-NOT

Persona Non Grata

Al sat in his car, parked
in front of your house, waiting
for you to discover the restrained

animal biding its time in the wilderness
of clothes that hung from his bones
like Spanish moss. I'm not saying

he loved you, just that he drove
by your house two, three times a night
and more on Saturdays, when you

and Sammybaby were steaming the windows in a '57
high-finned boat out on Limberlost Road.
Nor do I think he ever looked in the bay

window hoping to catch you. Once,
I sat with him for hours. It was Friday,
crickets were rubbing their legs together,

I was gabbing a mile a minute, and he asked
if I wouldn't mind sitting back and listening
to the night. He never put two words together.

He had to work at laughing, always
driving me or another guy out for a burger
or to crash a party, not to be friendly

but out of a code of obligation
that dictated his navigational chart.
We burned Marlboros down to their filters,

passed a bottle of wine and Kool Aid
back and forth. Sam's high-beams swept the windshield,
the lawn, and the driveway into daylight,

then died. I turned to the blank stare and smoke
and asked why he planted himself, night after night,
under a streetlight in a vegetable trance? He said,

I'm going to marry her with all the trimmings.
He opened the door for Sam, sucker-punched
his lights out, then came around the car

and marched you up the driveway, his hand
moving from shoulder to shoulder like a metronome
into the open garage. Now

you're divorced, your kids out of school
helping Al run a stamping plant, where Sammy
puts in his hours on a metal lathe. Last week,

when I was in town for my father's funeral,
Al and I went for a ride, two forty-year-old
misfires trying to find

something in common, something to do.
After I passed the open coffin, his eyes mortared shut
saying as much to me as they ever did, Al whispered

that if I wanted to see the lake or old friends,
he had his car. We pulled up
in front of your house, and while we passed

the evening and a joint between us, I remembered
asking you out once, in the early days
of Sam the man, for corned beef

and a coffee. Busy then; another time,
you said, smiling while walking
out of the cafeteria. I guessed that Al had somehow

gotten wind of it before the night of the punch
that sent Sam to the minor leagues, and I knew
that parking space would always be reserved,

like a table with a view at a lakefront
restaurant or a front row pew in the mortuary
chapel for smoky Al, Sam and lucky me.

Lovesong of the Spotted Touch-Me-Not

There was this fat
midnight bee: its succotash-
yellow hindquarters doing a samba
over the rose fluff
of joe-pye weed across from the bed

of moss in the woods where you
were scrutinizing the blue forking veins
of my right hand this morning,
the birthmark surprise between knuckles
flecked with bone-white mementos of burning

black polyethylene that stuck when I tried
to smother it in the crawl space
that grew into the spire of smoke
reaching for a sky that said,
so what, so there, and so long.

You whispered like a surgeon
through a sterile mask that I
have beautiful thumbs, the other one
having made a slow
descent from the prehistoric

arrowhead of your shoulder blade around the slope
of your belly and further
down to the elastic waistband, side-winding
through the no man's land
of gooseflesh, skidding

like a snapping turtle into the salt
marsh, into cool mud, where the tidal
rhythms of life begin to lap
and sway. Then you flipped the hand
over to the love and death lines

crisscrossing the blue
hole under skin
where a daydreamy pencil made
its mark in second grade, saying that sex
would interfere with your work.

So I wrote this
for the late afternoon, calling upon the conga
line of blood-swollen
mosquitos and the butter-sweet
goldenrod honey impacted in the comb

to support my case: Let's
disconnect the word processor
from the carotid artery, and move
our bedroll to a humid crack
in the world where the only

breeze comes off the wings of a hummingbird
taking sustenance and go shacky-wacky
thirty days and nights until the nearly
full moon finds us out, have a late supper,
then listen for the otherworldly

cry tearing the entrails
of a deer across the woods before sunrise.

A February Thaw Should Be Played Slowly

Where you dive, the six-sided
bits of sky, frozen

and angry, drive so hard
into the folded

pages of your eyes, they lift
you up like the white

wings of memory, the frost
heaving you back

into character, back
to me grieving by the light

of a seven-day candle, where we
can touch the little

growth of love we had almost
three years to scratch

the surface of between a father
and a son-in-law, and for that—

on this hill where it snows
almost every day, until summer suddenly

drives the roots of trees
into bedrock—I'm grateful.

Poet's Prayer

I received a form letter rejection
for someone else's manuscript, and that
meant a devoutly Christian woman
with a secret life, according to her poem
"Mata Hari Under the Table at the Last Supper,"
had likewise received bad news of my

anguished very late adolescent lapsed
Conservative Jewish meditation on the loss
of my foreskin at the hand of a bearded
old man, who took schnapps and a Cleveland
Hebrew salami for his trouble, while my mother
was pushed screaming into a cabinet laden

with shawls and a skullcap. The small
chapel where my father held
my hands and feet so the moil
could perform his tango of flesh
and razor has metamorphosed into an evening
ware boutique for the woman with extra

meat on her bones in the Great Synagogue
Theme Mall. My gentile
pen pal and I couldn't correspond enough
or get off the phone, so we started surprising
each other with a rhinestone fish
bottle opener from the holy land, shittimwood

carved into a crown of thorns, neon
everlasting light, pigs feet
fried in lard, and a gefilte fish kiwi tart. She

took hormones and turned her peach fuzz
into a Vandyke, migrating to an all-male
kibbutz, that picked kumquats and manufactured

goose down toilet seats, while I
had a sex change and converted
to Catholicism, joining an order
committed to prayer, song, and corresponding
with anyone who writes. She doesn't
anymore. I know I'm guilty of the sin

of pride, self-pity— I should send a picture
postcard of the convent, asking
what's new, but we never even
exchanged snapshots— and I don't want to blow
the flame out. I want to lie
low and tap the word

processor into the night, my bidirectional
printer spitting out hundreds of characters
every minute. And even if
I wake up not exactly
hung over from a little too much communion
wine taken on the sly—but not fit

as the fiddle of a friar
either—life waits,
my father always said, for no man,
woman, or beast. But
just last Friday, between a baked fish
and a tureen of fermented figs, a form letter

rejection appeared with a P. S. at the very
bottom that said, "These have torque. Please
send more." Joystick in hand, ready

for anything in my black-
and-white habit, the video monitor image
of my father's gravestone programmed

to stand up to an artillery barrage
of hands dotted with stigmata, I enjoy
the thousand delights of my cell
and a small beer, waiting
for my old friend in Israel to come around
and *The Succotash Review* to accept

my work— praying like a hundred and five
degree fever reaching for oblivion; praying
that this blister
of a world doesn't open like the saltwater
kiss of the Red Sea, swallowing every last
little magazine editor with a printing press. I'm not

praying for a mink
stole or to be a saint, just
to be published once. If You
can't handle that
one tiny mortal request, please pass
the buck to an old woods-queer ritual

circumcisor who knows how to finish a job
before it's too late, then clean his fingernails.
With the humility that befits my order, in the name
of The Holy Spirit, I am Sister
Hygenia, Painesville, Ohio, August, 1986:
Your servant.

Just Another Sunset

Tucked into a machine gun nest on the roof
of the Tel Aviv Hilton and staring

at the aquamarine hundred and ten degree
evening, I had

a waking dream of my overstuffed
grandmother falling like an immigrant

star into my arms. Isn't it
great, she said, staying up all night

in The Holy Land, and why don't you
ever write or send a picture?

If I were to fall
into her dream, I'd apologize and curl

like a chambered nautilus into what my
Uncle Pincus—his hands arcing

away from his chest—called
"the family bosom" and listen to her chant

names of her great
grandchildren, Sabbath prayers and imprecations

to eat the carrot floating between shimmering
yellow islands of schmaltz, while shards

of gossip blister the air around
aunts and cousins, and I swear on the sun

buried on the other side
of the planet, I'd never come out.

Your Lips, My Convalescence

"Fuck poetry," you said, "write me a novel."
The one promise I never kept. But here in bed,

plotless years into the future, my un-
repentant elbows straddle another
enemy of prose that wouldn't please you
looking over my shoulder as I look back
at a length of blanket over the length of me
and a catheter trailing like our friendship
out from under. I see your lips

open to the word "novel" then close
around cream cheese and a red
onion slice. And if I could wash my socks

in the sink down the hall I share with the running
bloodhound of your opinion
in pen and ink on the plaster, I wouldn't prop
the window on my fist and hurl
anathema down the street, at the end of which
you live out your life with my last chapter.

But here you are in a renaissance mood, a hopsack
of bread crumbs over your shoulder, on your way

to the park, where vendors' fingers twist balloons
into swords and flowers. You're up to your waist
in the pond—surrounded by the floating island

of your overcoat—and toss
your shirt like an earthbound bird trying to fly,
and shoot it down with the crossbow
of your suspenders. I grab

a corner of a nearby bench, wondering
why half our lives we harm
each other with intent. I give up and roll
a cigarette, bum a match from a drifter, who lights
a newspaper torch circling
you scattering bread crumbs into the night

of strays that come
on the backs of animals, in the arms of neighbors,
in slings and carriages, by wing
and by word of mouth. Like the swirling
nebulae of your graffiti,

they come to me smoking on a bench
or spread-eagled on the bed

where you bend
over my concentration, curious still
why anyone would bother, my answer
turning to your open-mouthed

mirage: my fever, my inquisitor.

Lovesong of the Pale Touch-Me-Not

While you search for white
specks of satellite on an easy path,
crickets and faraway freeway
noises cry out below
fieldstone walls that disappear into woods
or wander like the shadow of extinct

earthbound birds winding their way
back to us climbing Bear Hill, climbing
into a memory of my father's voice, years
after the "Red Scare" and "Yellow Peril,"
frightened, and warning me not to say
"communist" over the phone. A line

from Nadezhda Mandelstam's *Hope Abandoned*
stirs another picture of my father
in suspenders trying not to hear
my sister crying on his knee, while he watched
the news from his overstuffed, yellow chair.
"Real idiots in the clinical sense

are a godsend," she said, thinking
of an editor in Kiev, one of the last
to give her husband work. Then you slide your long
fingers into my back pocket, asking
what I like about your personality. I swear
I couldn't separate the moonstruck

distillation of your radiance
from the sudden gooseflesh. Your teasing
pushes me into the oval office, where the president,

cleansed of cancer from nose to rectum,
daydreams of citizens on the ground
floor of a Berkeley hills detention camp,

on their stomachs, their fingers
interlaced behind their necks, a helicopter
searchlight lashing. I remember you
holding a flashlight, while I fiddled
with the double-carbureted failure of my
'66 Volvo, crimson and silent as a prehistoric

insect blocking your driveway.
Looking down the honeycomb of the radiator,
I could see my father dispensing with my services
and politicians carrying on the ancient grinding
of the human spirit. I needed you and loved you
loving me back, struggling with spark plugs

and a difficult divorce under the sly
hood of that old car that would die
a sentimental death rusting
into oblivion. Now that I love you
even more, even
more than the firefly of your wildness driving

my imagination faster and higher
through the moonlit perfume
of marsh milkweed and wild asters
where we take our pleasure and our time smoking
out the stubborn
satellite in each of us, then let them go

on their separate missions, coming down the hillside,
pale and weightless and shivering a little.

Barn Cat Summer

for Mark Cox

Sometimes I climb the silo
on a full-moon night, tie myself
and a six-pack to the top rung, smoke
and drink one after another and slowly
scrutinize the flickering details
until I can see the water-swollen
satellite in the amber bottle and lob it
high over the corncrib's
horizon of slats alive with raccoon shadows.
Under the cover of a temporary
stillness I never want to come out from,
that sickly sweetness when a wingspread
white owl drops out of the dark
and I know
I can say the thing that makes
every beer-bellied, chain-smoking
hump of self-pity as quietly
beautiful as a butterfly drying its wings,
then apologize to the bullfrogs
for the interruption, my skin
prickling with love for the humid night, love
for my heartsick vegetarian,
who built a funeral pyre for a peacock, then
smelled the flesh and ate
the thing down to its fragile
skeleton—love waiting for love's
apparition to appear in her nightshirt and say
Come down before you break your neck, all
that endless arguing and I can't
remember what sent me nowhere

you could see from a silo, foolish
one, her voice disintegrating
into beer-glass fireworks over pissed-off
coons, frightened and careening
into brush, the sparking sunrise
end of my cigarette sailing after them as I
say Don't come back but if you do
I've got two little twist-top darlings left,
one for the bad guy of your dreams, one
for you if you can catch it.

About the Author

Roger Weingarten grew up in Cleveland, Ohio. He earned a BA from
Goddard College and an MFA from the University of Iowa. He has
received an Ingram Merrill Award, fellowships from the Dana Founda-
tion, a National Endowment for the Arts Creative Writing Fellowship,
and three Vermont Council for the Arts Individual Artist grants. He is
the author of seven books of poetry and the co-editor of three poetry
anthologies. His poems have appeared in magazines aroud the country,
including *A.P.R., Poetry, The New Yorker, The New Republic, The Kenyon
Review, Antaeus,* and *The Sewanee Review.* He teaches in, and directs, the
MFA in Writing Program at Vermont College.

Infant Bonds of Joy

was set in 11 point Adobe Garamond and designed on the Macintosh.
Adobe Garamond is a revival of the famous Garamond typefaces based
on recastings of sixteenth-century type designer Claude Garamond's orig-
inal metal versions. The Adobe version was designed by Rob Slimbach of
Adobe Systems.

This book was printed and bound by Maple-Vail Book Manufacturing
Group, Binghamton, New York. It was designed by Lucinda Hitchcock.